T0043173

Who Was
Ulysses S. Grant?

by Megan Stine

illustrated by Mark Edward Geyer

Penguin Workshop

For my sister Dolores—MS

For my wife, Marianne, and my children, Alan and Anna
—MEG

PENGUIN WORKSHOP
An Imprint of Penguin Random House LLC, New York

If you purchased this book without a cover, you should be aware that this book is stolen property. It was reported as "unsold and destroyed" to the publisher, and neither the author nor the publisher has received any payment for this "stripped book."

Penguin supports copyright. Copyright fuels creativity, encourages diverse voices, promotes free speech, and creates a vibrant culture. Thank you for buying an authorized edition of this book and for complying with copyright laws by not reproducing, scanning, or distributing any part of it in any form without permission. You are supporting writers and allowing Penguin to continue to publish books for every reader.

The publisher does not have any control over and does not assume any responsibility for author or third-party websites or their content.

Text copyright © 2014 by Megan Stine.
Illustrations copyright © 2014 by Penguin Random House LLC. All rights reserved.
Published by Penguin Workshop, an imprint of Penguin Random House LLC, New York.
PENGUIN and PENGUIN WORKSHOP are trademarks of Penguin Books Ltd.
WHO HQ & Design is a registered trademark of Penguin Random House LLC.
Printed in the USA.

Visit us online at www.penguinrandomhouse.com.

Library of Congress Control Number: 2014017366

ISBN 9780448478944   15 14

Contents

Who Was Ulysses S. Grant?....................................1

A Boy Who Loved Horses............................4

To West Point...18

Love and War...25

Married but Alone.......................................38

Civil War..47

Winning the War...65

Lincoln Is Shot...77

President Grant...83

Rich and Poor...92

Timelines..104

Bibliography..106

Who Was
Ulysses S. Grant?

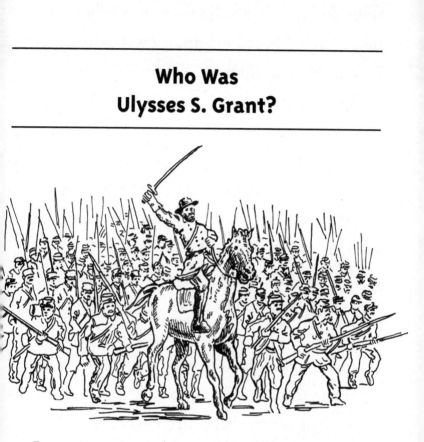

It was a summer day in 1861. The Civil War—
the clash between Northern and Southern states—
was just beginning. A Northern officer, Colonel
Ulysses S. Grant, was getting ready to lead about
a thousand men into battle. That's what he'd been

trained to do. He had been an army officer for many years. He had fought in a war before.

But this was different. This was the first time Ulysses was in charge. It was the first time he was leading a huge group of men to fight—and possibly die.

As Ulysses marched along, he began to get nervous. He later wrote that his heart pounded so hard, he could feel it in his throat.

The closer he got to the Southern troops, the more frightened Ulysses became. Secretly, he wished he could stop marching. But he couldn't do that. It was his job to keep going, no matter what happened next.

And guess what happened next: Ulysses found the enemy soldiers' campsite. But the soldiers were gone! They had run away!

All at once, Ulysses realized something. The enemy soldiers had been just as afraid of him as he was of them.

From that day on, Ulysses S. Grant never let fear stand in his way.

By the time the war ended in 1865, Ulysses S. Grant was a hero—more popular than anyone in the country, even more popular than Abraham Lincoln, the president of the United States!

War made him a hero, and yet he hated war all his life.

Chapter 1
A Boy Who Loved Horses

A baby was born on April 27, 1822, in a tiny one-room house in Point Pleasant, Ohio. For almost a month, his parents weren't sure what to call him. Finally, they put a bunch of names in a hat. Then the baby's father drew out a name—Ulysses! It was the name of a famous hero and warrior from the past.

The baby's father decided to name him Hiram Ulysses Grant. But everyone called him Ulysses.

Ulysses's father was Jesse R. Grant. Jesse was a big talker and a show-off. He liked to brag. From the moment Ulysses was born, Jesse bragged about what a great baby his son was.

Jesse owned a tannery—a business that turned animal skins into leather. It was smelly, messy, and disgusting. Ulysses hated it. He was willing to do any job, as long as he didn't have to work in his father's tannery.

Ulysses's mother was Hannah Simpson Grant.

Like most women in those days, she didn't work outside the home. Hannah was very quiet—almost silent. She hardly ever spoke.

When Ulysses was a year old, his family moved to Georgetown, Ohio. They needed a

bigger house. More children were coming along.
Ulysses had a brother, Samuel. Then three sisters
and another brother were born.

From an early age, Ulysses loved horses. When he was two years old, his father took him to the circus. The ringmaster asked if anyone in the audience wanted to ride the circus horse. The first

boy who tried was thrown off. Ulysses begged
and begged to ride. Finally his father said yes.
So off Ulysses went, riding around the circus ring.
A huge smile spread across his babyish face.

When he was five years old, he learned how to ride on a horse's back— standing up!

Both of Ulysses's parents loved him and treated him with kindness. They never scolded him or punished him. They gave him a lot of freedom to go fishing and swimming. But they also

expected him to do many chores. Ulysses used horses to haul firewood and plow the fields.

Ulysses also tamed horses. Neighbors paid him to break in horses that were too hard to handle. He could ride faster than any of the other boys in town.

One day, when he was eight years old, he saw a horse he wanted to buy. Ulysses's father decided to let Ulysses make the deal all by himself. His father told Ulysses to offer the horse's owner twenty dollars, and if he wouldn't take that, to offer him twenty-two fifty. And if he wouldn't take that, then Ulysses could offer him twenty-five dollars.

Ulysses spoke to the horse's owner. But instead of bargaining, he blurted out the truth. "Papa says I may offer you twenty dollars for the colt, but if you won't take that, I am to offer twenty-two and a half, and if you won't take that, to give you twenty-five."

Of course the man got the highest price for the horse! When the story got around town, everyone laughed except Ulysses. He was embarrassed about it for years.

During the winter, Ulysses went to school. The
school was a one-room schoolhouse. Children
of all ages were taught at the same time. Ulysses
was good at math, but the school didn't have any
algebra books. Jesse Grant worried that Ulysses

was not learning enough. So he came up with an
idea: send the boy to West Point!

West Point was a famous military academy
in New York. It was known for training army
officers. The school had a good math department.
And best of all, it was free!

But when Jesse told his son that he was going to West Point, Ulysses said, "I won't go!" Ulysses had no desire to be in the army—none at all.

Jesse said, "I think you *will* go."

Ulysses knew what that meant. He was going to West Point whether he wanted to or not.

Chapter 2
To West Point

Ulysses had never seen a train before. Now he was riding one to West Point, New York. The train went eighteen miles an hour—so fast he couldn't believe it!

The military school sat on the bluffs high above the Hudson River. Large gray stone buildings looked out over the water. It was a beautiful place.

When Ulysses arrived, he reported to the officer in charge. But Ulysses's name wasn't on the list of new students. The officer was expecting someone named Ulysses S. Grant—not Hiram Ulysses Grant. The paperwork was wrong—but the officer wouldn't correct it! The army had its rules.

So Ulysses gave in. He took the name West Point insisted on. It stuck for the rest of his life.

Pretty soon, he met his classmates. They looked at his initials and laughed. Was his name U. S. Grant? Did that stand for United States Grant? Or Uncle Sam Grant? His friends started calling him "Sam" for short.

Ulysses loved the beautiful campus, but he didn't like the military life. He hated marching and doing drills. He couldn't imagine becoming a soldier after graduation.

As for his classes, he wasn't good at much of anything except math. He hardly ever studied. Instead, he went to the library and took out novels. He liked to lie in his room reading them. But by his second year, he was fitting in better at West Point. And then West Point started a new class—horseback riding! Ulysses was already a pro with horses. He offered to break in the new, wild

horses. Everyone was impressed with his skills.

But in his last year at West Point, Ulysses did something terrible. He lost his temper and hit a horse. He'd never done anything like that before. He loved horses. He was punished severely and could have been kicked out of school.

However, in June 1843, Ulysses S. Grant did graduate. Now what?

Like all graduates of West Point, he was required to serve four years in the army. He hoped to be put in the cavalry with the soldiers who rode horses. But having hit a horse was a black spot on his record. The cavalry was not likely to take him—even though he was easily the best rider West Point had ever seen. If he didn't get into the cavalry, he would have to take the infantry— the foot soldiers.

So Ulysses went home to Ohio and waited for his orders. He wouldn't know his fate until a letter arrived.

Chapter 3
Love and War

Infantry!

When the letter arrived, Ulysses was very disappointed. His orders were to report to St. Louis, Missouri, home to the biggest military post in the country. He had no choice but to get his new uniform and go.

But at least now Ulysses was an officer. It meant he had more free time. So one day, he rode out to visit the family of his roommate from West Point, Fred Dent.

FRED DENT

The Dent family was warm and welcoming.

The younger children loved Ulysses. The parents invited him to come often, so he did. Ulysses enjoyed the visits except for one thing: The family enslaved people. Some were forced to work in the Dent House as servants while others worked out in the fields of the large plantation.

Ulysses had always hated slavery. His whole family did. Ulysses and Mr. Dent would never agree about the subject of slavery.

One day the Dents' oldest daughter, Julia, returned home. She had been away visiting friends. Ulysses had never met her before. Julia was eighteen years old, and just like Ulysses, she loved to read. And she loved to ride horses. She

JULIA DENT

could ride almost as well as he could! Julia was the main reason Ulysses kept visiting the Dent family.

Then one day in May 1844, new orders came. Ulysses was to leave immediately for Louisiana with his troops.

Ulysses didn't want to go. He hadn't realized it until now, but he was in love with Julia!

As fast as he could, Ulysses rode toward her house. At one point, he and his horse had to cross a swollen stream and were almost carried away! But Ulysses had a rule for himself: never turn back. Finally, Ulysses made it, soaking wet, to the Dents'. Wearing baggy clothes borrowed from one of Julia's brothers, Ulysses told Julia exactly how he felt. Happily, she felt the same way!

Ulysses gave Julia his class ring from West Point, as a sort of engagement ring. Then he went off to Louisiana to join his troops.

Ulysses didn't know it yet, but the United States was about to enter a war. And he would be right in the middle of it.

For the next year, Ulysses and his fellow soldiers camped in Louisiana. The campsite was near the border with Texas. But Texas wasn't a state yet. It was its own nation.

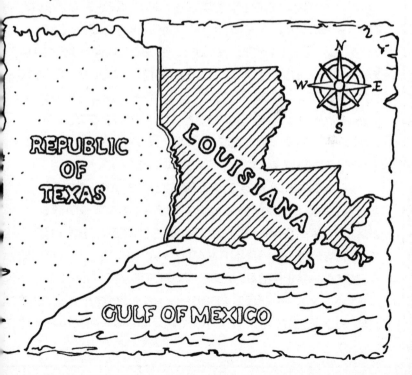

THE MEXICAN-AMERICAN WAR

IN THE EARLY 1800S, THE AREA WE NOW CALL TEXAS WAS A BIG OPEN SPACE. MEXICO HAD ALREADY SETTLED PARTS OF IT. AMERICANS MOVED IN AND BEGAN TO SETTLE OTHER PARTS. THE MEXICANS THOUGHT ALL OF TEXAS BELONGED TO THEM. THE AMERICAN SETTLERS FOUGHT A WAR WITH MEXICO—AND WON. AT THE END OF THE WAR, THE SETTLERS FORMED THEIR OWN COUNTRY, CALLED THE REPUBLIC OF TEXAS.

THE REPUBLIC OF TEXAS WANTED TO BECOME PART OF THE UNITED STATES. CONGRESS AGREED. TEXAS BECAME A STATE IN 1845. BUT HOW BIG WAS TEXAS? WHERE WERE THE BOUNDARIES? THAT WAS THE QUESTION. MEXICO STILL CLAIMED PART OF THE TERRITORY. SO THE UNITED STATES SENT THE ARMY TO THE BORDER, TRYING TO PROVOKE A FIGHT. THEY WANTED A WAR WITH MEXICO—BUT THEY WANTED MEXICO TO START IT.

IT WORKED. MEXICAN SOLDIERS ATTACKED AMERICAN SOLDIERS. NOW THE UNITED STATES COULD SAY THAT MEXICO HAD STARTED THE WAR.

ULYSSES S. GRANT SAID THAT HE THOUGHT THE MEXICAN-AMERICAN WAR WAS ONE OF THE MOST UNJUST WARS EVER FOUGHT. HE BELIEVED AMERICA HAD NO RIGHT TO TRY TO TAKE LAND FROM MEXICO.

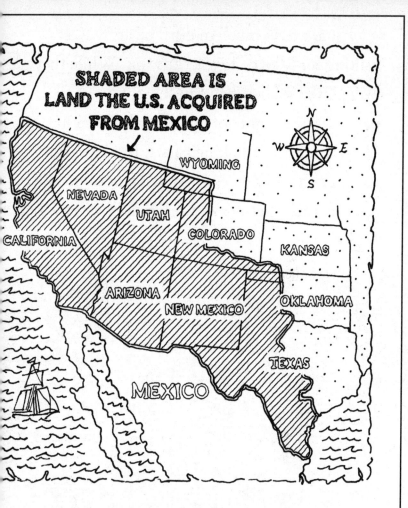

WHEN THE WAR WAS OVER, THE UNITED STATES
SIGNED A TREATY—AN AGREEMENT—WITH MEXICO.
MEXICO AGREED TO GIVE UP TEXAS, CALIFORNIA,
NEVADA, NEW MEXICO, ARIZONA, UTAH, AND PARTS
OF COLORADO AND WYOMING. IN RETURN, THE
UNITED STATES PAID MEXICO $15 MILLION.

There wasn't much to do. The army was waiting for Mexico to start the war. While they waited, the soldiers had fun. Ulysses went to parties in the homes of families who lived nearby. He also took up smoking cigars. In the warm months, the soldiers enjoyed being outside. When winter came, they got to work building rustic huts to live in.

Meanwhile, Ulysses wrote to Julia often, saying how much he missed her.

In the fall, Ulysses and his troops were sent from Louisiana into Texas. The following year, in April 1846, they moved into a part of Texas that Mexico claimed as its own.

The business of war was about to begin.

Ulysses was a second lieutenant. He watched how the older officers behaved. Some generals were harsh and worked the men too hard for no reason. Other generals were show-offs who bragged about themselves. One famous general named Winfield Scott strutted around in his fancy uniform so soldiers would notice him.

GENERAL WINFIELD SCOTT

But Scott treated the Mexican villagers well. Even though the United States was at war with Mexico, Scott wouldn't let his soldiers take food or property from townspeople. The soldiers had to buy it, and pay a fair price.

Ulysses admired Scott's fairness. But he admired General Zachary Taylor even more. Taylor wore plain clothes—not his fancy uniform. He was firm but kind to his men. Even in the face of danger, General Taylor remained calm. Here was the kind of general Ulysses wanted to be.

The Mexican-American War lasted almost two years. Most of that time was spent marching

GENERAL
ZACHARY TAYLOR

on foot to battle sites. Or building roads so US troops could reach enemy locations. Or finding mules to carry food and supplies.

Much less time was spent fighting the enemy. One battle near San Antonio lasted only thirty minutes!

The most dangerous day for Ulysses came during the Battle of Monterrey, when his troops were running out of ammunition. In order to get more supplies, someone had to ride past the enemy. Ulysses volunteered and found a way to protect himself from the Mexicans firing at him.

He didn't sit on the saddle! Instead, he put only one foot in the stirrup, and hung on to the side of his horse. That way, he was shielded from gunfire. Luckily, both the horse and Ulysses were safe.

The fighting in Mexico finally ended in the fall of 1847.

At last, Ulysses could return to Missouri and Julia. He couldn't wait!

Chapter 4
Married but Alone

Ulysses and Julia had waited four long years to get married. Their wedding was held on August 22, 1848.

The next day, they left to visit his family in Ohio. A few weeks after that, Ulysses had to report for duty once again.

Ulysses had never planned to stay in the army, but now he seemed to have no choice. How else could he make a living? The next few years were miserable. The army sent him from one place to another. At first, he was stationed in Detroit, Michigan, and Julia came along.

But military life was hard for Julia. So when Julia got pregnant, she decided to go back home to St. Louis to have the baby. A boy was born on May 30, 1850. Julia named him after her father: Frederick Dent Grant.

Ulysses couldn't wait to see his new son. He asked for leave and rushed to St. Louis. Right away he loved being a father and adored playing with his child. The sad part was saying good-bye and heading back to his army post.

Soon Ulysses was sent to distant army posts

in Oregon, San Francisco, and other parts of
northern California. There was no way Julia and
the baby could manage the long, difficult journey
to the West Coast. Besides, he didn't have enough
money to pay for their trip.

For two years, from 1852 to 1854, Ulysses
was alone in the Pacific Northwest. The Grants'

second baby was born on July 22, 1852. Julia named him Ulysses S. Grant Jr. Everyone called him "Buck." Ulysses didn't even know the baby had been born until nearly five months later!

Ulysses's job in the army was dreary. He was in charge of ordering and handing out supplies.

Often he just sat in his room, alone, writing letters to Julia. Sometimes Ulysses got bad headaches—so bad he could hardly do any work at all.

Lonely and bored, Ulysses began to drink too much alcohol. Soldiers often drank together, but Ulysses was different. Even one or two drinks made him drunk. The officer in charge thought Ulysses had a big problem, and said so. This hurt Ulysses's reputation for years to come.

Finally, in April 1854, Ulysses decided to quit the army. Enough was enough. He couldn't stand to be away from his family any longer.

Back in Missouri, near the Dents, Ulysses farmed land that Julia's father gave them. He built a log cabin for his family. But the house was so plain, Julia hated it. And the crops weren't worth much. Ulysses named his farm "Hardscrabble." The word means hard work that doesn't give much in return for the effort.

After four years of hardscrabble living, Ulysses was ready to quit farming. For the next few years,

he worked for a company that rented out properties. But he was too softhearted. When people couldn't pay their rent, Ulysses let them stay for free. Finally he moved the family to Galena, Illinois. His father owned a leather-goods store there. Ulysses went to work as a clerk. But he wasn't happy there, either. He didn't fit in with the business world.

The only joy Ulysses had came from his family. He and Julia had four children now. Ellen, their daughter, was born in 1855. They called her Nellie. Their youngest son was born in 1858. They named him Jesse, after Ulysses's father.

Ulysses was thirty-eight years old in 1860. Nothing he had tried his hand at so far had succeeded—except the army. He was no good at farming, no good at business.

Ulysses didn't know it, but the course of history—as well as the course of his own life—was about to change forever. The Civil War would soon begin, and Ulysses S. Grant—who never wanted to be a soldier—would become a key figure in the eventual victory for the North.

Chapter 5
Civil War

As soon as Ulysses heard that war was starting, he wanted to return to the army. He thought he was needed. And the war might put an end to slavery once and for all.

The Northern states didn't have a large army. President Lincoln had asked for seventy-five thousand new volunteers.

Ulysses was willing to help out. Like everyone else in Galena, he rushed to a meeting about the war. He hoped to be in charge of a whole regiment—a group of more than a thousand men— in the volunteer army.

PRESIDENT BRAHAM LINCOLN

WHAT STARTED THE CIVIL WAR?

THE CIVIL WAR WAS ALSO CALLED THE WAR BETWEEN THE STATES. IT WAS A WAR FOUGHT OVER STATES' RIGHTS AND SLAVERY. PEOPLE IN THE SOUTHERN STATES ENSLAVED PEOPLE AND WANTED TO KEEP IT THAT WAY. PEOPLE IN THE NORTHERN STATES WERE AGAINST SLAVERY. THEY WANTED IT TO END. SOUTHERNERS FELT PEOPLE IN NORTHERN STATES HAD NO RIGHT TO TELL THEM WHAT TO DO.

AS NEW STATES JOINED THE UNION, THE ISSUE OF SLAVERY HEATED UP. WOULD THE NEW STATES BE FOR OR AGAINST ENSLAVING PEOPLE? IN THE FIRST HALF OF THE 1800S, SEVERAL DIFFERENT LAWS ABOUT SLAVERY WERE PASSED TO TRY TO KEEP PEACE BETWEEN NORTH AND SOUTH. BUT LINCOLN'S ELECTION AS PRESIDENT IN 1860 WAS THE FINAL STRAW FOR THE SOUTH. THE SOUTHERN STATES KNEW THAT LINCOLN WANTED TO END SLAVERY. WITHIN WEEKS

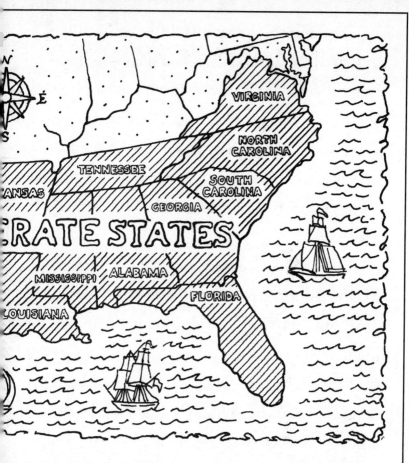

OF HIS ELECTION, THE SOUTHERN STATES STARTED
TO PULL OUT OF THE UNITED STATES. THEY WERE
FORMING THEIR OWN COUNTRY. THEY CALLED IT
THE CONFEDERATE STATES OF AMERICA.

WHEN THE SOUTH ATTACKED FORT SUMTER
IN SOUTH CAROLINA ON APRIL 12, 1861, THE CIVIL
WAR BEGAN. IT LASTED FOUR YEARS, AND LEFT
MORE THAN SEVEN HUNDRED THOUSAND MEN DEAD.

The volunteer army was different from the regular army. The soldiers could choose their own officers—by a vote. Ulysses was not elected. Sometimes officers were appointed by the governor of the state. But Ulysses was not appointed.

Ulysses's next step was to write to Washington, asking to be made a colonel. No one answered his letter.

It looked like no one wanted U. S. Grant. Maybe the army remembered the stories about his drinking. Maybe they didn't want a man like that in charge of other men's lives.

That didn't stop Ulysses. He worked hard to organize volunteer soldiers. After a while, the men around him saw that Ulysses could be trusted.

The governor of Illinois put him in charge of a wild, unruly regiment. Ulysses remembered General Zachary Taylor and tried to be the same kind of leader. Ulysses was firm but always fair. The men quickly learned to respect him.

In just over a month, Ulysses was promoted to general—and he hadn't even been in battle yet!

But in the eastern half of the United States, early battles were being fought—and the South was winning. Southern generals seemed to be more organized and determined than Northern ones. One famous Southern general got the nickname "Stonewall" Jackson because he stood like a stone wall against the Northern attack. The most famous Southern general of all was Robert E. Lee. Lee was so confident, he even had plans to invade the North!

GENERAL STONEWALL JACKSON

The Northern generals had what Abraham Lincoln called "the slows." They didn't have enough fight in them; they preferred to avoid battles. President Lincoln needed a general to take charge of the Union army and fight to win the war.

ROBERT E. LEE

THE MOST FAMOUS GENERAL OF THE CONFEDERATE STATES WAS ROBERT E. LEE. A BRILLIANT COMMANDER AND THE SON OF A REVOLUTIONARY WAR OFFICER, LEE HAD BEEN A TOP STUDENT AND GRADUATE OF WEST POINT. IN 1852, HE BECAME THE HEAD OF WEST POINT.

WHEN THE CIVIL WAR BEGAN, LEE WAS OPPOSED TO IT. HE DIDN'T WANT THE UNION TO BREAK UP. BUT WHEN PRESIDENT LINCOLN ASKED LEE TO BECOME THE GENERAL OF THE UNION ARMY, LEE CHOSE TO FIGHT FOR HIS HOME STATE OF VIRGINIA INSTEAD. HE COULDN'T TURN AGAINST THE SOUTH. HIS FAMILY HAD LIVED IN VIRGINIA FOR CENTURIES.

NORTHERN GENERALS WERE AFRAID OF LEE AND THOUGHT HE WAS SUPERHUMAN. BUT ULYSSES S. GRANT FELT DIFFERENTLY. "I HAD KNOWN HIM PERSONALLY," GRANT SAID, "AND KNEW THAT HE WAS MORTAL."

Perhaps U. S. Grant was the general Lincoln was looking for. In November 1861, on his own, Ulysses led his men to attack a rebel camp in Belmont, Missouri. At first, it seemed like an easy victory. The Confederate soldiers ran away. But Ulysses's men started to celebrate too soon. The enemy had time to come back and surround them. Now they were trapped!

Ulysses refused to surrender. He led his men to an escape route, fighting all the way. U. S. Grant was learning about war not from books but from actual battles.

THE BORDER STATES

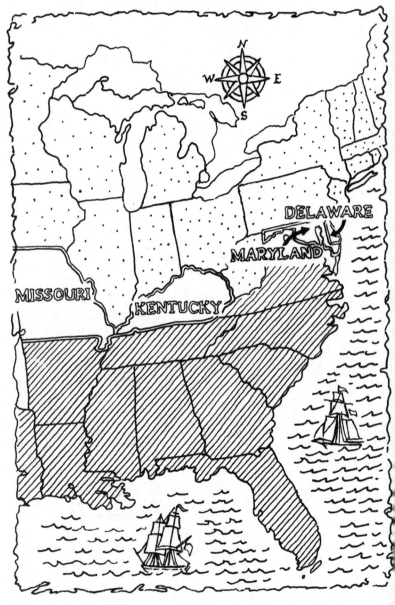

DURING THE CIVIL WAR, SOME STATES WERE STUCK BETWEEN THE NORTH AND THE SOUTH. THEY WERE CALLED THE BORDER STATES. IN THESE STATES, SOME FAMILIES ENSLAVED PEOPLE. MISSOURI, WHERE JULIA DENT'S FAMILY LIVED, WAS A BORDER STATE. IT WAS ONE OF FOUR STATES WHERE SLAVERY WAS ALLOWED THAT NEVER PULLED OUT OF THE UNION. THE OTHER THREE WERE DELAWARE, KENTUCKY, AND MARYLAND.

KENTUCKY TRIED TO STAY OUT OF THE WAR BY CLAIMING IT WAS "NEUTRAL." THAT MEANT KENTUCKY WOULDN'T TAKE SIDES IN THE WAR. BUT KENTUCKY WAS IN THE DIRECT PATH THAT THE NORTHERN ARMY NEEDED TO TAKE TO GET TO THE SOUTH. SO ULYSSES MARCHED HIS TROOPS INTO KENTUCKY AND TOOK CONTROL OF AN IMPORTANT TRANSPORTATION LOCATION. AFTER THAT, THE GOVERNMENT OF KENTUCKY WAS WILLING TO JOIN THE UNION SIDE.

Although he hated war, Ulysses was good at it. He could always picture how a battlefield was laid out—and how to win.

He had another advantage, too. Ulysses knew a lot of the Southern officers he was fighting against. Some had been at West Point with him. Many had fought with him in Mexico. Ulysses knew their weaknesses and strengths. He knew how they thought. He knew whether they were brave or not.

In February 1862, Ulysses was sent to attack Fort Donelson, an important Confederate fort in Tennessee. One of the enemy generals in charge was a man named General Pillow. Ulysses knew him. Like his name, Pillow was a softy—not willing to fight hard.

GENERAL PILLOW

Ulysses captured the fort easily. Pillow and the other Southern generals hoped that Ulysses would let them off easily. After all, they had known Grant for years.

But Ulysses wrote a letter that made him famous. In the letter, he said he would only accept one thing: "unconditional surrender." That meant the Southern army had to give up without any promises of going free.

After that, people started calling Ulysses "Unconditional Surrender" Grant. His initials—U. S.—were the same as the first letters of those words!

Now that he was winning battles, Ulysses was promoted again. He was made a major general! The newspapers wrote about Ulysses. When people read that Ulysses S. Grant liked cigars, they sent boxes of them to him at headquarters. He smoked them all the time.

But the war dragged on and on. It was terrible.

One of the biggest, bloodiest battles that Ulysses took part in came at the beginning of the second year of the war. It was the Battle of Shiloh in Tennessee in April 1862. When it was over, Ulysses said it was possible to walk all the way across a field, stepping only on dead bodies—without ever stepping on the ground.

In the end, Ulysses won the Battle of Shiloh. But more than nineteen thousand Union and

Confederate soldiers were killed or wounded in two days.

The night after the first day of the battle, Ulysses was sitting outside in the rain. He was cold and hungry. He walked inside a house where wounded men were being treated. But the sight was so terrible, he quickly left. It was easier staying out in the rain at night than watching young men having arms and legs cut off.

The wounded men often were carried off the battlefield to nearby houses. Private homes were often turned into hospitals—whether the owners liked it or not.

When people read newspaper stories about Shiloh, they were shocked. Everyone blamed Ulysses at first. The cost of victory was too high. Some powerful men in Washington wanted President Lincoln to fire Ulysses. Even Mary Lincoln, the president's wife, called Ulysses a butcher.

MARY LINCOLN

Lincoln listened thoughtfully to the complaints. But he understood that the war would take a long time to win. And it would cost many hundreds of thousands of lives. When one politician urged him to fire Ulysses, Lincoln was very quiet. Then he looked up. "I can't spare this man," Lincoln said. "He fights."

Chapter 6
Winning the War

In October 1863, Ulysses was put in charge of almost half of the Union army. The war had dragged on for over two and a half years. Now Ulysses realized he was going to have to change his plan of attack. At the outset of the war, he wouldn't let his soldiers take food from the people in the South. He ordered his men to respect their property and treat the local citizens well. He wanted to be fair to the enemy, the way General Scott had been in Mexico.

But after the Battle of Shiloh, Ulysses changed his mind. His men were too hungry—and he needed them to be healthy. Otherwise, how could the North win the war? He let his men take food, clothing, and everything else the army could use.

He ordered the soldiers to destroy anything that the Confederate army needed in order to continue the war.

They destroyed railroads and factories that helped produce things that the Southern army needed.

**GENERAL
GEORGE MEADE**

A major turning point for the war came in July 1863. A Union general named George Meade defeated General Robert E. Lee at Gettysburg, Pennsylvania. The very next day, Ulysses S. Grant defeated the Southern army at Vicksburg, Mississippi. The war wasn't over yet—it would last almost two more years. But the Southern army never regained its full strength after that.

In March 1864, President Lincoln asked Ulysses to come to Washington, DC. In a ceremony at the White House, the president put Ulysses in charge of the entire Union army! He was named a lieutenant general. The only other soldier ever given that title was George Washington.

One of the ways Ulysses planned to win the war was by capturing Southern railroads and cutting off other forms of transportation. He knew the Southern army couldn't survive long without new supplies of food, men, and ammunition.

Still, the war went on for another year. Fifty thousand Union soldiers were killed or injured in May 1864. In one earlier battle in 1862

at Antietam, Maryland, more than thirteen thousand men were killed or wounded in a single morning!

Ulysses sent General William T. Sherman across Georgia to the city of Atlanta. When Sherman's men reached Atlanta, they burned the whole city down. Then they burned down plantations as they marched toward the sea.

After that, Ulysses sent troops to Richmond, Virginia, the capital of the Confederate States. Soon the people of Richmond fled.

Finally, it looked like General Robert E. Lee's troops were beaten. The South had lost the war. Ulysses sent Lee a letter saying that it was time for Lee to surrender.

Ulysses waited in a farmhouse near Appomattox, Virginia, for a reply. He was having one of his very bad headaches. He spent the night putting hot treatments on his neck, hoping that would help.

The next day, Grant received a note from Lee agreeing to surrender. Instantly, his terrible headache went away!

The two famous generals met on April 9, 1865, at the home of a man named Wilmer McLean. Ulysses, who never liked to wear his fancy uniform, arrived in muddy clothes and dirty boots. Robert E. Lee was dressed in his best, cleanest, most impressive uniform. His buttons were shiny and new. Ulysses, however, was the man who had won the war. Lee looked good, but he had lost, and everyone knew it.

As always, Ulysses was fair and kind. He talked in a warm, friendly manner with Lee for the first few minutes. They both remembered that they had fought together in the Mexican-American War.

Finally, Lee said that they should write down
the terms of the surrender. Ulysses was generous.
He could have demanded that all the Southern
soldiers give up their horses. He could have taken
all their weapons. He could have insisted on
taking Southern soldiers as prisoners. Instead, he
said the soldiers could keep their personal pistols
or swords. He said they could keep their horses.

He knew the men would need them, after the war, for farming. He also made sure the Confederate soldiers had food. Most of them were starving.

Lastly, Ulysses ordered the Union army to stop firing their guns in celebration. He understood his soldiers were excited that the war was over. But it wasn't right to rub it in. "The rebels are our countrymen," Ulysses said. Southerners were no longer the enemy. The North and South were one nation again.

Chapter 7
Lincoln Is Shot

A few days after Lee surrendered, Ulysses went to Washington to see the president. Julia and their young son Jesse came, too. The war was nearly over. Everyone in Washington was celebrating.

The next evening, President Lincoln invited Ulysses and Julia to join him and Mrs. Lincoln to see a play at Ford's Theater. Ulysses knew Julia

FORD'S THEATER

disliked the president's wife and did not want to attend. So Ulysses politely said no.

Instead, the Grants and Jesse headed by train to New Jersey to spend time with the rest of the children. But when the train stopped in Philadelphia, a man came rushing to Ulysses.

President Lincoln had been shot at the theater!

Ulysses rushed back to Washington. By the time he got there, President Lincoln was dead.

The whole country fell into a state of mourning. The man who shot Lincoln— John Wilkes Booth—had

JOHN WILKES BOOTH

planned to stab Ulysses that night, too. Why?

John Wilkes Booth was a Southerner. He bitterly hated the men who had beaten the South.

To the end of his life, Ulysses regretted not being at Ford's Theater that night. He always believed he could have saved the president's life had he been there.

With Lincoln dead, the vice president became the president. His name was Andrew Johnson.

Ulysses didn't admire President Johnson. Johnson wasn't good-hearted like Lincoln. He didn't want formerly enslaved people to have the vote. He felt more sympathy for the enslavers than he did for the people who were enslaved. But at least the war was over.

ANDREW JOHNSON

During a victory parade that marched past the White House, Ulysses sat beside President Johnson.

The parade lasted for two days! The line of soldiers was thirty miles long. Soldiers kept calling out Ulysses's name. "Grant! Grant!" they shouted. President Johnson didn't like it one bit.

From then on, everywhere he went, Ulysses was mobbed. Friends and admirers got together and bought him three houses—as gifts! One fancy house was in Philadelphia. A smaller house was in Galena, Illinois. The third house was in a very pretty neighborhood in Washington, DC. People

from all over the world sent him gifts of china, silver, swords, and cigars.

As a high-ranking general in the army, Ulysses would have a $21,000 per year income until he died. That was a lot of money back then. Ulysses was now forty-three years old. He wasn't a young man, but he still had a lot of life ahead of him.

What would he do with it?

Chapter 8
President Grant

For the first few years after Lincoln's death, Ulysses continued as general of the army. He lived in Washington, but he tried to stay out of politics.

It was a difficult time for America. The country was trying to come together again. People wanted a leader they could trust—someone like Ulysses. They wanted someone who was fair and even-handed. They wanted someone who respected the rights of Black people. President Johnson was not that man.

In 1868, they asked Ulysses to run for president.

Ulysses was tempted to run, for the good of the country. But there was one big problem: money. If he gave up being general of the army, he would lose his lifelong income. Yes, he would make $25,000 a year as president. But that was only for four years, or maybe eight years if he was elected twice. Then what? By then, he would be an old man, and have almost no income. He didn't want to be poor again.

Ulysses didn't exactly say yes, he'd run for president. But he didn't say no. In May 1868, the Republicans chose him to be their candidate for president. Ulysses wasn't even at the convention in Chicago when he was nominated. He found out when Edwin Stanton, the secretary of war, told him!

A few weeks later, Ulysses and Julia went back to Galena. Campaigns for president were very different back then. Ulysses wasn't expected to make speeches or meet voters. All he had to do was sit home for the next few months and wait. He was happy to do that.

On election night, Ulysses walked up the hill

to the house of a friend. The telegraph company had run a line into the friend's house. That way, Ulysses and a few other men could sit there all night, smoking cigars, while the election results came in on the telegraph wires. Finally, at two in the morning, the results became clear. Ulysses walked home and found Julia waiting for him. "I am afraid I am elected," he told her.

When Ulysses was sworn in as president on March 4, 1869, he, Julia, and their two youngest children, Nellie and Jesse, moved into the White House. Right away, Julia and Ulysses began making changes. The White House had become run-down and shabby. Julia decorated the house and cleaned it up.

She also made new rules for the staff. They couldn't hang around in their old clothes, smoking cigarettes and playing cards. They had to dress in dark suits and wear white gloves. They worked for the president of the United States, after all!

Ulysses made changes of his own. In the past,

people had been allowed to just walk into the White House and try to catch the president for a conversation. Ulysses put secretaries in charge, so the White House ran more like an office.

But Ulysses didn't want to be separated from the people. He went out for walks in Washington almost every day—alone. For fun, he liked to race through the streets in a carriage, driving his horses as fast as he could.

Julia loved living in the White House. She had parties and open houses every week. She hired a chef to cook all the meals, instead of using an army cook.

As president, Ulysses was both a success and a failure. He supported voting rights and civil rights for African Americans. He sent the army to arrest members of the Ku Klux Klan—a group of hateful white men who did not believe that Black people deserved to be free. They wore white robes and hats to hide their faces, and they went out at night to scare, whip, and attack formerly enslaved people. He also

helped keep the peace after the war. His slogan during the election was "Let us have peace." And he meant it. When General Sherman wanted to go out west and kill all the Native Americans, Ulysses tried to make peace with them instead.

But Ulysses also made many mistakes. He had never been a good businessman. He couldn't tell when someone was being sneaky. It turned out that many men in his administration were dishonest. Some took bribes and stole millions of dollars in tax money. When the news came out, people found it hard to believe that Ulysses hadn't known what was going on.

Nevertheless, in 1872, U. S. Grant was reelected president. At the end of his second term, some people wanted Ulysses to run for a third term. But he wanted no part of it. Julia, however, was heartbroken over his decision. She loved the White House and never wanted to leave. Ulysses couldn't wait to get out.

Chapter 9
Rich and Poor

What Ulysses wanted to do, after leaving the White House, was travel. He had never been to Europe. But could the Grants afford it? Once again, Ulysses and Julia were broke. All the money he had earned as president was gone. They had spent most of it just running the White House. And the rest Ulysses had given away to anyone who asked.

Luckily, there was still one source of income. Ulysses had bought shares in a silver mine, and suddenly the silver mine hit it big. Ulysses and Julia decided to travel while they could afford it.

In May 1877, they sailed for England. There they met Queen Victoria and had dinner at Windsor Castle. For the next two years, Ulysses,

Julia, and their son Jesse traveled to nearly every country in Europe. Then they went on to Egypt, Turkey, the Middle East, India, and China. From there, they sailed to Japan. Everywhere they went, they met with kings and queens. Ulysses was honored and treated like a hero.

When the money began to run out and Julia was tired of traveling, they sailed home. Huge crowds gathered to see Ulysses as he docked in San Francisco. In Chicago, an enormous parade was held in his honor. Afterward, Ulysses met the

famous author of *The Adventures of Tom Sawyer*,
Mark Twain. The two men soon became friends.

For a short time, Ulysses and Julia went to live
in their house in Galena. But now that they had
seen so much of the world, the small town bored

them. So when some rich friends offered Ulysses enough money to buy a house in New York City, he happily accepted it.

Life in New York was glamorous—and expensive. Ulysses's oldest son, Buck, was twenty-nine years old now and a businessman. He introduced Ulysses to his partner, Ferdinand Ward. Ward was a Wall Street investor. He promised big profits if Ulysses would invest in his company. It seemed like a good deal, so Ulysses handed over all his money. He also told all his friends and family to invest in the company called Grant and Ward. For a few years, everyone seemed to make money.

But then suddenly, it all fell apart. Ward ran off with everyone's money, and left Ulysses to clean up the mess. The investors—his friends, his family, and many old soldiers—were ruined.

Ward was caught and sent to prison for ten years. Ulysses was left penniless and deeply embarrassed. Everyone knew he and Buck

FERDINAND WARD

had been fooled by Ward. But that didn't make him feel any better.

To make matters worse, Ulysses was sick. His throat hurt him all the time. When he finally went to his doctor in February 1885, it was too late. He had cancer from the cigars he had smoked all his life. He had only a few months to live.

Now he was broke and dying. How would Julia and Jesse survive after he was gone?

Years before, Mark Twain had suggested that Ulysses write his memoirs—the story of his life. Now it seemed like the only way to earn some money for his family. Mark Twain offered to publish the book himself. He promised to give Ulysses a much better deal on the profits than any other publisher would offer.

So for the next several months, Ulysses sat in a chair in his New York City apartment and wrote his life story in pencil. Meanwhile, Mark Twain sent out ten thousand men who went door to door telling people about the book and getting them to put in an order for it. Many of the salesmen were old soldiers. They wore their Union army uniforms. More than 150,000 people ordered the book in advance.

In his final weeks of life, Ulysses sat on a porch in a cabin in the Adirondack Mountains, writing. He was in a lot of pain, but he wanted to finish

the book. When soldiers learned he was there, they marched past the house and saluted in tribute to him. Ulysses would just look up from his writing and wave. Then he got back to work.

Finally the book was completed. A few days later, on July 23, 1885, Ulysses died. Julia and their four children were at his bedside. He was sixty-three years old.

When the country learned of his death, church bells chimed everywhere. They chimed sixty-three times. The funeral held in New York City was the biggest the city had ever seen. Four famous generals from the Civil War—two from the North, and two from the South—helped carry his casket. The funeral march wound through the city for hours, with a parade of mourners seven miles long. Soldiers from both the Union and Confederate armies rode together in carriages.

In death, Ulysses had done what he had tried to do in life—bring the nation together in peace.

Ulysses was buried in a temporary tomb in Riverside Park in New York City. Twelve years later, a huge marble tomb was built as a monument to his greatness. When Julia died in 1902, she was buried there beside him—his lifelong love and best friend. Now they were together forever.

TIMELINE OF
ULYSSES S. GRANT'S LIFE

1822 — Ulysses S. Grant is born Hiram Ulysses Grant on April 27 in Point Pleasant, Ohio

1839 — Attends West Point
Adopts the name Ulysses S. Grant

1843 — Graduates West Point and becomes an officer in the army

1848 — Marries Julia Dent

1850 — The Grants' first child, Frederick Dent Grant, is born

1854 — Quits the army and returns to his family

1860 — South Carolina secedes from the Union

1861 — Mississippi, Florida, Alabama, Georgia, Louisiana, Texas, Virginia, Arkansas, North Carolina, and Tennessee secede from the Union
Civil War begins
Ulysses S. Grant returns to the army as a volunteer to fight in the Civil War

1864 — President Lincoln appoints Grant as lieutenant general

1865 — General Robert E. Lee surrenders, ending the Civil War

1869 — Ulysses S. Grant is sworn in as president of the United States on March 4

1872 — Reelected president

1885 — Writes his memoirs
Ulysses S. Grant dies at sixty-three years old

TIMELINE OF
THE WORLD

The Missouri Compromise establishes slavery-free—1820
territory in the United States

Slavery is banned in the British Empire—1833

Queen Victoria marries Prince Albert—1840

New York City establishes the first official—1845
police department

The United States and Mexico sign the Treaty of—1848
Guadalupe Hidalgo, ending the Mexican-American War
Discovery of gold in California sparks a gold rush

Harriet Tubman escapes to freedom—1849

Harriet Beecher Stowe's *Uncle Tom's Cabin* is published—1851

The first transatlantic telegram is sent—1858

Congress authorizes the building of a—1862
transcontinental railroad

The Thirteenth Amendment to the United States—1865
Constitution ends slavery in the United States

Louisa May Alcott writes *Little Women*—1868

The Transcontinental Railroad is finished—1869

The Fifteenth Amendment to the Constitution gives—1870
African American men the right to vote

Alexander Graham Bell is awarded the patent—1876
for the telephone

Thomas A. Edison develops the first practical lightbulb—1879

Mark Twain's *Adventures of Huckleberry Finn* is published—1884

BIBLIOGRAPHY

Grant, Ulysses S. **Memoirs and Selected Letters**. New York: The Library of America, 1990.

* Marrin, Albert. **Unconditional Surrender: U.S. Grant and the Civil War**. New York: Atheneum, 1994.

Perret, Geoffrey. **Ulysses S. Grant: Soldier & President**. New York: Random House, 1997.

Simpson, Brooks D. **Ulysses S. Grant: Triumph Over Adversity, 1822–1865**. Boston: Houghton Mifflin Company, 2000.

* Books for young readers